Scan Me to Connect

Copyright

This book is a work of nonfiction. The author has made every effort to ensure the accuracy of the information presented herein. However, the author assumes no responsibility for errors or omissions. Any use of this information is at the reader's discretion and responsibility.

About the Author

Pablo Puig is a recognized expert in cloud strategy and deployment in China, with a proven track record of helping global organizations thrive in one of the world's most complex cloud ecosystems. Since 2019, Pablo has supported over 40 international enterprises in navigating the regulatory, operational, and technical challenges of building and optimizing cloud environments in China. His clients span a wide range of sectors including finance, healthcare, manufacturing, and e-commerce each with unique compliance requirements and infrastructure needs.

His journey into China's cloud market began when one of his clients a European software company struggled for months to deploy their cloud workloads in the region. Pablo stepped in, resolved the regulatory bottlenecks, and helped the company go live within four weeks. That pivotal moment sparked a deep commitment to demystify cloud computing in China and support others facing the same roadblocks.

As a cloud consultant, strategist, and educator, Pablo has delivered tailored solutions on Microsoft Azure, AWS, Alibaba Cloud, Tencent Cloud, and hybrid architectures for multinational companies entering the Chinese market. He's also a frequent speaker at international conferences and webinars, where he shares practical insights on cloud compliance, data residency, and cloud-native development strategies within China's unique legal and technological environment.

Pablo is the author of four definitive guides:

- *AWS China: The Complete Guide*
- *Azure China: The Complete Guide*
- *Cloud Computing in China*
- *DeepSeek: Revolutionizing AI*

Each book is built on hands-on experience, real-world case studies, and a mission to simplify cloud adoption for IT professionals, cloud architects, and business leaders operating in or expanding into China.

With Azure China: The Complete Guide, Pablo offers a practical, step-by-step playbook tailored to professionals looking to deploy or scale their Azure workloads in compliance with Chinese regulations. Packed with examples, workarounds, and hard-earned lessons from the field, this book is designed to be your essential companion for cloud success in China.

Table Of Contents

CHAPTER 1
INTRODUCTION TO AZURE IN CHINA

Lesson 1

The History of Azure in China

Partnership with 21Vianet	Azure China Official Launch	Major Capacity Expansion	Two New Azure Regions	Expansion into Hebei
2013	2014	2017	2018	2022

The history of Microsoft Azure in China is a story of pioneering collaboration, adaptation, and strategic partnerships that exemplify how global technology leaders navigate the unique challenges of the Chinese cloud market. Azure, Microsoft's cloud platform, officially entered China in 2014, establishing itself as the first international public cloud service to be operated independently by a local provider. This move marked a significant milestone in China's cloud computing history and showcased Microsoft's commitment to expanding its footprint in one of the world's fastest-growing digital economies.

Azure's entry into China was facilitated through a partnership with 21Vianet, a leading Chinese carrier-neutral internet data center services provider. This collaboration allowed Microsoft to comply with China's strict regulatory environment, which mandates that foreign cloud providers work with local entities to deliver cloud services. By licensing its technology to 21Vianet, Azure was able to operate under China's legal framework while maintaining its global standards for reliability, performance, and innovation.

The launch of Azure in China was a calculated response to the country's burgeoning demand for cloud services. The rapid growth of China's digital economy, fueled by e-commerce, mobile internet, and the adoption of artificial intelligence, created an urgent need for robust, scalable, and secure cloud platforms.

Azure's entry into this market addressed a critical gap, offering enterprises a trusted global cloud solution tailored to China's regulatory and operational realities.

Over the years, Azure's presence in China has evolved significantly. The platform began with data centers in Beijing and Shanghai, operated by 21Vianet, and has since expanded to include additional regions and availability zones. This growth reflects Microsoft's ongoing investment in the Chinese market and its dedication to meeting the needs of local and multinational enterprises operating in the region. Azure in China has also introduced a range of services that align with global offerings while adapting to local requirements, ensuring compatibility with Chinese regulations and customer expectations.

One of the key factors driving Azure's success in China has been its commitment to compliance and security. Microsoft and 21Vianet have worked closely with Chinese authorities to obtain certifications and ensure that Azure adheres to the country's stringent data residency and cybersecurity laws. This approach has not only built trust with customers but also positioned Azure as a reliable partner for businesses navigating the complexities of China's regulatory landscape.

As the first global cloud provider to establish a foothold in China, Azure has paved the way for other international players, setting a benchmark for how to operate effectively within this unique market. Its history is a testament to the importance of local partnerships, cultural understanding, and a commitment to innovation in driving success in the Chinese cloud industry. For businesses and IT professionals, Azure's journey in China offers valuable lessons on adapting to local conditions while leveraging global expertise to deliver world-class cloud solutions.

Lesson 2

21Vianet Blue Cloud

T o operate legally within China's heavily regulated cloud environment, foreign cloud providers are required to collaborate with licensed local partners. For Microsoft Azure, that partner is 21Vianet Group, Inc. — one of China's leading carrier-neutral and cloud-neutral internet data center service providers.

Founded in 1999 and publicly traded on the NASDAQ (VNET), 21Vianet is widely recognized for its robust network infrastructure, regulatory compliance expertise, and strategic role in facilitating the entry of global technology companies into the Chinese market. With operations in more than 20 cities across China, the company offers a broad suite of services, including internet data center (IDC) services, enterprise cloud hosting, and business-grade VPN services. Its clientele includes a wide range of industries, from internet giants and government agencies to blue-chip multinational corporations and agile SMEs, serving over 6,000 enterprise customers.

The partnership between Microsoft and 21Vianet, which began in 2013, allows Azure to be delivered under local licensing and operational control, ensuring that all services comply with Chinese cybersecurity laws, data residency requirements, and telecommunications regulations. Under this model, 21Vianet is responsible for the operation and delivery of Azure services in China, while Microsoft provides the technology, engineering support, and product roadmap. This arrangement not only enables Azure to legally operate in China but also gives customers the confidence that their cloud infrastructure is managed by a local partner with deep knowledge of the region's technical and legal environment.

It also ensures that Azure China can scale with demand, respond quickly to market-specific needs, and remain aligned with the strict regulatory expectations of the Chinese government.

By combining Microsoft's global cloud expertise with 21Vianet's local presence, data center infrastructure, and compliance track record, this partnership represents a blueprint for how international cloud services can operate successfully within one of the world's most challenging but opportunity-rich digital markets.

For more information about 21Vianet, visit: https://en.21vbluecloud.com/

Lesson 3

Understanding the Chinese Cloud Market

T he Chinese cloud market is one of the fastest-growing and most dynamic in the world, fueled by the rapid digital transformation of industries, government initiatives, and an increasingly connected population. For Microsoft Azure, entering and thriving in this unique environment required not only technological excellence but also a profound understanding of the market's specific characteristics, challenges, and opportunities.

China's cloud computing sector is shaped by a combination of local business practices, government regulations, and consumer expectations. The demand for cloud services in the country has been driven by industries such as e-commerce, gaming, finance, and manufacturing, all of which rely on robust, scalable, and compliant cloud infrastructure to remain competitive. Azure has played a pivotal role in meeting these demands by providing a secure and flexible platform that supports innovation and growth.

A defining feature of the Chinese cloud market is its strict regulatory framework. Laws such as the Cybersecurity Law and the Data Security Law impose stringent requirements on data storage, processing, and cross-border transfer. For businesses leveraging Azure in China, compliance with these regulations is not optional; it is a fundamental requirement for operating within the country. Azure's partnership with 21Vianet ensures that its cloud offerings adhere to these local laws, providing customers with confidence in their compliance and security.

The Great Firewall, which governs internet access in China, further shapes the cloud market. This regulatory structure limits access to global websites and services while prioritizing the development of domestic internet infrastructure. Azure's services in China are isolated from its global regions, enabling businesses to comply with data residency requirements while still benefiting from Microsoft's advanced technologies. However, this isolation also necessitates unique architectural considerations, such as the use of local APIs and integration with domestic services, which Azure supports through its tailored offerings.

Despite these challenges, the Chinese cloud market presents immense opportunities. Government-led initiatives, such as the "Digital China" strategy, encourage digital transformation across sectors, creating demand for advanced cloud solutions. Azure has capitalized on these opportunities by introducing services tailored to industries with high growth potential, such as artificial intelligence for manufacturing and analytics for retail.

Another critical aspect of the Chinese cloud market is its competitive landscape, dominated by domestic giants such as Alibaba Cloud, Tencent Cloud, and Huawei Cloud. These local providers have deep market knowledge and established customer bases, posing significant competition for global players like Azure. However, Azure differentiates itself through its integration with global enterprise ecosystems, its focus on hybrid cloud solutions, and its adherence to international standards for security and performance.

For IT professionals and enterprises considering Azure in China, understanding the market's intricacies is crucial. Success requires not only leveraging Azure's technological capabilities but also adapting strategies to align with local norms and regulations. By understanding the dynamics of the Chinese cloud market, businesses can unlock the full potential of Azure to drive innovation, enhance efficiency, and achieve sustainable growth in one of the world's most promising digital economies.

Lesson 4

Azure Regions and Availability Zones in China

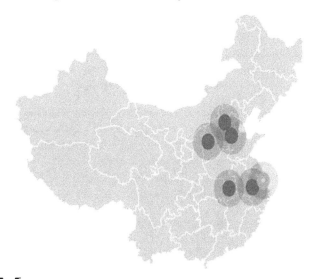

Microsoft Azure's presence in China is a cornerstone of its global cloud strategy, designed to meet the needs of a rapidly growing market with unique regulatory and operational challenges. Operated by 21Vianet, Azure China delivers a range of services tailored to the local environment while leveraging Azure's globally trusted infrastructure and technology. This collaborative approach ensures that Azure China adheres to strict data sovereignty and cybersecurity requirements, allowing businesses to operate with confidence in one of the most regulated cloud markets in the world.

Azure China operates three primary regions: China North (Beijing), China East (Shanghai), and the recently launched China North 3 (Hebei). These regions are strategically located to serve diverse geographic areas and industries, enabling businesses to access scalable, reliable cloud infrastructure. The addition of China North 3, located in Hebei Province, represents Azure's commitment to scaling its operations in response to growing demand.

This region offers three Availability Zones, providing enhanced resilience for businesses that rely on high availability and disaster recovery. The launch of China North 3 also underscores Microsoft's dedication to investing in China's cloud infrastructure, ensuring that businesses have access to state-of-the-art resources to support their operations.

Each of these regions has been strategically developed to serve specific business needs while supporting local compliance mandates. However, access to these regions is not uniform. As of now, China North (Beijing) and China East (Shanghai) are restricted to legacy customers only. All new customers must deploy their workloads in China North 3, located in Hebei Province, just 150 km from Beijing. China East 3 (Shanghai) is a hidden region which can only be used for China North 3 (Hebei)'s DR site.

Here is a summary of Azure China's current regions and their Availability Zones:

Region	Availability Zones	Location
China North 1	1 Zone	Beijing
China North 2	1 Zone	Beijing
China North 3	3 Zones	Hebei
China East 1	1 Zone	Shanghai
China East 2	1 Zone	Shanghai
China East 3	1 Zone	Shanghai

Azure China regions are entirely isolated from the global Azure infrastructure. This isolation is mandated by China's regulatory framework and ensures that all data processed or stored in Azure China remains within its borders. While this isolation guarantees compliance, it introduces challenges for multinational businesses seeking to integrate Azure China with their global operations. Unlike global Azure regions, Azure China regions cannot directly communicate with global Azure services or regions, necessitating workarounds such as VPNs or secure data gateways to enable cross-border operations.

To maximize the benefits of Azure China, businesses should adopt a multi-region strategy. Deploying workloads across regions such as China North, China East, and China North 3 can significantly enhance fault tolerance and disaster recovery capabilities. Tools like Azure Traffic Manager enable intelligent traffic routing, ensuring users are connected to the nearest or most efficient region. This is particularly critical for enterprises in industries like e-commerce and gaming, where performance and user experience are paramount.

Overall, the structure of Azure China, with its regions and availability zones, is designed to support the unique operational and regulatory needs of businesses in the country. As the cloud landscape continues to evolve, staying informed about these geographical considerations will empower IT professionals and business leaders to make informed decisions. By leveraging the capabilities offered by Azure China, organizations can enhance their agility, ensure compliance, and drive innovation in an increasingly competitive market.

Lesson 5

Considerations for Hosting Services in Hong Kong

Hosting services in the Azure Asia Pacific (Hong Kong) region presents unique opportunities and challenges for businesses catering to users in mainland China. Unlike Azure China regions, which are operated independently by 21Vianet under local regulatory frameworks, the Azure Hong Kong region is part of the global Azure infrastructure managed directly by Microsoft. This distinction makes it a strategic choice for businesses looking to serve both global and regional audiences, but it requires careful consideration of performance, compliance, and operational factors.

The Hong Kong region is often utilized as a gateway for businesses expanding into Greater China. Its proximity to mainland China offers reduced latency compared to hosting services in other global Azure regions. However, it is not directly connected to Azure China, meaning that businesses must account for the Great Firewall, which regulates and sometimes restricts cross-border internet traffic. For companies delivering content, applications, or services to Chinese users, this can lead to slower response times and potential disruptions.

From a compliance perspective, hosting services in Hong Kong does not fulfill mainland China's strict data residency and cybersecurity requirements. Chinese laws mandate that sensitive data such as personal information or critical data must be stored and processed within mainland China. As a result, businesses using Azure Hong Kong for operations involving regulated data expose themselves to legal risks and potential service interruptions. For this reason, the Hong Kong region is better suited for hosting non-sensitive services, global-facing applications, and data that do not fall under Chinese regulatory oversight.

Despite these challenges, Azure Hong Kong can play a pivotal role in a hybrid deployment strategy. Many organizations choose to host their core applications and data in Azure China to meet compliance requirements while using Azure Hong Kong for global connectivity and integration with non-China operations. By combining the strengths of both regions, businesses can achieve a balance between performance, compliance, and scalability.

For example, an international e-commerce company looking to expand its operations in Greater China deployed its product catalog and customer engagement tools in Azure Hong Kong, while storing customer data and processing transactions in Azure China. This setup allowed them to maintain compliance with Chinese data laws while ensuring fast-loading pages and global integration. By leveraging Azure ExpressRoute to establish a dedicated and secure connection between the two regions, they mitigated latency issues and improved overall user experience.

Ultimately, the decision to host services in Azure Hong Kong should be based on the nature of the business, the type of data being handled, and the specific needs of end-users. Businesses that plan their deployment strategies with these factors in mind can effectively navigate the complexities of hosting services in this region while achieving their operational goals.

Lesson 6

Setting Up an Account in Azure China

Setting up an account in Azure China is a process that differs significantly from what global Azure users are accustomed to. Unlike the self-service, console-based registration used globally, Azure China operated independently by 21Vianet requires an invitation to begin account creation. This invitation-only approach is a direct result of China's regulatory landscape, which imposes strict controls on foreign cloud services operating within its borders.

For international organizations looking to expand into China, this initial barrier often proves to be a source of delay and confusion. One such case involved a European technology company eager to establish its cloud environment in China. After weeks of unanswered emails and stalled progress with Azure China's support team, they turned to me for assistance. Drawing on my network and experience navigating the local system, I facilitated contact with the right stakeholders within the Azure China team. Within just one week, they received the formal invitation required to proceed, enabling them to launch their environment and meet their internal project deadlines.

This scenario is not uncommon. Many foreign companies underestimate the importance of local relationships in China's cloud ecosystem. Having supported numerous clients through this process, I can say with certainty that establishing local connections and engaging with a qualified advisor or Azure partner can significantly streamline your onboarding experience.

Once the invitation is secured, businesses can proceed with the account registration. This step requires specific documentation and local representation, including:

- Chinese Legal Entity Name
- Chinese Business License
- Chinese Contact Person Information (Full name and phone number)

These requirements reflect China's emphasis on data sovereignty and accountability, particularly for foreign enterprises. Only entities with a valid Chinese business registration can open an Azure China account.

From a contractual standpoint, there are 2 options:

- Direct OSPA (Online Service Premium Agreement): Customers sign directly with 21Vianet for a 3-year term, handling billing and support through 21Vianet.
- Indirect OSPA (Online Service Premium Agreement): Customers engage through a partner, signing a commercial contract with the partner and an OSPA with 21Vianet. Billing is managed by the partner, while 21Vianet provides support.

	Direct OSPA	**Indirect OSPA**
Agreements	Customer signs an OSPA Agreement package directly with 21V.	Customers signs a commercial contract with partner, and an indirect OSPA Agreement with 21V
Agreement duration	3 years	3 years
Billing and payment	Customers pays directly to 21V.	Customers pays to indirect partners
Support	21V Supports	21V support except billing, which is supported by partners

Because of these differences, account setup in Azure China is not just a technical step, it's a strategic process. Businesses should invest time in evaluating which subscription model aligns with their growth goals, compliance obligations, and budget forecasts. They should also factor in legal support to review contracts and understand operational responsibilities in the local jurisdiction.

In parallel, it is highly recommended that new customers engage Azure China's partner ecosystem. Local partners and system integrators can provide critical services during onboarding, including identity verification, legal compliance, resource provisioning, and architectural planning.

These experts help bridge the gap between Microsoft's global design principles and the specific expectations of Chinese regulators and infrastructure realities.

In summary, the process of setting up an account in Azure China is not immediate or universal but it is highly achievable with the right preparation, guidance, and expectations. Understanding the invite-only nature, the regulatory prerequisites, and the payment structure are essential to ensuring a successful and compliant cloud journey. By partnering with trusted local advisors and being proactive about documentation and strategic planning, businesses can navigate the onboarding process smoothly and lay a strong foundation for long-term success in the Chinese market.

Lesson 7

Creating an Azure China Trial Account

For businesses looking to evaluate Azure China before committing to a long-term contract, Microsoft through its local operator 21Vianet offers a trial account option. This trial is designed to give organizations hands-on experience with the platform, allowing them to test services, validate compatibility, and assess performance in China's unique cloud environment.

Unlike global Azure trials, the Azure China trial is not self-service. It must be requested and processed through official channels and takes approximately 3 to 4 working days to be activated. This trial offering has proven to be a decisive factor for many of my clients who were assessing multiple cloud providers before making their final decision.

Each Azure China trial account includes:

- $500 USD equivalent in service credit (converted into RMB)
- Access to core Azure services for testing and proof-of-concept deployments
- A 2-month duration, after which the account can be upgraded to a paid subscription

The following documentation must be submitted in order to request an Azure China Trial Account:

- Chinese Legal Entity Name
- Chinese Business License
- Chinese Contact Person Information (including name and phone number)

These prerequisites reflect China's data sovereignty and security regulations, which apply equally to trial accounts. Only businesses with a valid Chinese business registration can access trial services. In my experience, helping clients set up these trial accounts has often been the turning point in the cloud vendor selection process. Once clients are able to deploy workloads, test network latency, explore the Azure China portal, and validate service availability, they gain the technical clarity and confidence needed to move forward.

CHAPTER 2

KEY DIFFERENCES BETWEEN AZURE CHINA AND AZURE GLOBAL

Lesson 1

Portal, Domains, and Endpoints

Understanding how portals, domains, and endpoints work in Azure China is essential for any business planning to operate in the region. While the overall user experience in Azure China might appear similar to that of global Azure, the underlying infrastructure is completely separate. Azure China is operated independently by 21Vianet under Chinese regulatory oversight, which means that the service environment including the management console, domain structure, authentication endpoints, and APIs is isolated from the global Azure infrastructure.

Users cannot log into the Azure China environment using global Azure accounts. Azure China requires a dedicated tenant created through the China-specific portal: https://portal.azure.cn, whereas global Azure users access resources through https://portal.azure.com. This separation ensures that all authentication, provisioning, and data handling stays within China, in compliance with its cybersecurity and data localization laws.

Domains used within Azure China also reflect this separation. For example, authentication requests are handled through login.partner.microsoftonline.cn rather than login.microsoftonline.com, which is used globally. Likewise, when managing resources or using APIs, users must interact with endpoints like management.chinacloudapi.cn instead of management.azure.com. Even storage endpoints differ, with Azure China using domains such as *.blob.core.chinacloudapi.cn instead of *.blob.core.windows.net. These small but significant differences are critical in application development, DevOps automation, and API integrations. Failure to adjust endpoint references when deploying global applications into China often results in authentication errors, broken services, or unexpected behavior.

Endpoints for identity, storage, networking, and compute services must all be reconfigured to match the China-specific structure. For instance, Microsoft Graph API requests must go to microsoftgraph.chinacloudapi.cn, and Azure Active Directory API calls should target graph.chinacloudapi.cn.

Developers need to be diligent about using the correct endpoints during deployments, SDK configurations, or infrastructure-as-code scripts. Real-world deployment scenarios have shown that global templates copied into Azure China environments without modification often fail until these endpoint differences are addressed.

One international customer I supported had developed a globally consistent CI/CD pipeline using Azure DevOps and Microsoft Graph APIs. When they began expanding operations into China, their authentication and provisioning scripts broke because they hadn't adjusted for the China-specific endpoints. Once we reviewed the domain and endpoint mappings, made the necessary updates, and redeployed their templates, the environment provisioned correctly within Azure China. These seemingly small changes often make the difference between a successful deployment and a complete service outage.

In practice, the separation of portals, domains, and endpoints is not just a technical distinction, it's a regulatory requirement. It guarantees that all data, authentication, and platform control remains within China's jurisdiction. But for businesses, this means extra configuration, duplicate infrastructure management, and custom logic within applications to ensure environment awareness. For example, developers may need to implement conditional logic in their apps to detect whether they're operating in global Azure or Azure China, and then dynamically select the appropriate endpoints and authentication flows.

Ultimately, a deep understanding of how Azure China's portals, domains, and endpoints differ from global Azure is foundational for any cloud deployment in the region. It impacts everything from network design and API integration to security policies and DevOps workflows. By planning for these differences early in your architecture and development lifecycle, your organization can avoid costly deployment delays, maintain compliance, and ensure seamless operations in one of the world's most regulated and isolated cloud environments.

Lesson 2

Azure in China Account Sign-in

Another key operational difference between Azure China and global Azure lies in how users authenticate and sign in to their accounts. Because Azure China is a sovereign cloud environment operated by 21Vianet, it uses a separate identity system, isolated from the Microsoft global directory. This affects everything from how users log into the Azure portal to how administrators manage resources via CLI or PowerShell.

For IT professionals and developers managing infrastructure programmatically, it's essential to understand that commands and authentication flows differ slightly when connecting to Azure China. Most command-line tools, such as Azure PowerShell and Microsoft Graph PowerShell, require users to explicitly set the correct environment for Azure China during sign-in.

The following table highlights the differences in sign-in syntax between Azure Global and Azure China, using common PowerShell modules as examples:

Sign in Description	Azure Global	Azure in China
Sign in to Azure with an authenticated account for use with Azure Resource Manager	Connect Azure Account	Connect Azure Account Environment Azure China Cloud
Sign in to Microsoft Entra ID with Microsoft Graph PowerShell	Connect mgGraph	Connect mgGraph Azure Environment China
Sign in to your Azure classic portal account	Add Azure Account	Add Azure Account Environment Azure China Cloud

Failing to specify the correct environment will lead to authentication errors or the inability to access resources within Azure China. These commands ensure that your session is properly scoped to the China region, allowing for full compatibility with Azure Resource Manager (ARM), Microsoft Graph, and classic Azure services provisioned through 21Vianet.

For organizations managing both global and Chinese environments, this distinction also reinforces the importance of scripting and automation practices that are environment-aware. Including conditional logic in your infrastructure-as-code templates and scripts to differentiate between Azure environments will help prevent configuration drift and access issues.

Understanding these sign-in differences is a small but essential part of operating reliably in Azure China. It's another example of how this region, while powered by Microsoft's technology stack, requires localized knowledge and precise operational adjustments.

Lesson 3

Azure China Endpoints

T he table below lists API endpoints in Azure Global vs. Azure in China for accessing and managing some of the more common services.

Service Category	Azure Global	Azure China
Azure (in general)	windows.net	chinacloudapi.cn
Microsoft Entra ID	https://login.microsoftonline.com	https://login.chinacloudapi.cn
Azure App Configuration	azconfig.io	azconfig.azure.cn
Azure compute	cloudapp.net	chinacloudapp.cn
Azure data	https://{location}.experiments.azureml.net	https://{location}.experiments.ml.azure.cn
Azure storage	blob.core.windows.net	https://management.chinacloudapi.cn/
Azure management	https://management.azure.com/	https://management.chinacloudapi.cn/
Azure service management	https://management.core.windows.net	https://management.core.chinacloudapi.cn
Azure Resource Manager	https://management.azure.com	https://management.chinacloudapi.cn

Azure portal	https://portal.azure.com	https://portal.azure.cn
SQL Database	database.windows.net	database.chinacloudapi.cn
Azure Service Bus	servicebus.windows.net	servicebus.chinacloudapi.cn

Azure SignalR Service	service.signalr.net	signalr.azure.cn
Azure Time Series Insights	timeseries.azure.com	timeseries.azure.cn
Azure Access Control Service	accesscontrol.windows.net	accesscontrol.chinacloudapi.cn
Azure HDInsight	azurehdinsight.net	azurehdinsight.cn
Azure Service Fabric cluster	cloudapp.azure.com	chinaeast.chinacloudapp.cn
Azure Spring Cloud	azuremicroservices.io	microservices.azure.cn
Microsoft Entra ID	onmicrosoft.com	partner.onmschina.cn
Microsoft Entra logon	https://login.microsoftonline.com	https://login.partner.microsoftonline.cn
Microsoft Graph	https://graph.microsoft.com	https://microsoftgraph.chinacloudapi.cn
Azure AI services	https://api.projectoxford.ai/face/v1.0	https://api.cognitive.azure.cn/face/v1.0
Azure Bot Services	botframework.com	botframework.azure.cn
Azure Key Vault API	vault.azure.net	vault.azure.cn
Azure Container Apps Default Domain	azurecontainerapps.io	No default domain is provided for external environment.

Lesson 4

Service Availability

When planning cloud deployments in China, it's crucial to recognize that Azure China, operated by 21Vianet, does not offer the same breadth of services as global Azure. This discrepancy arises from China's regulatory landscape and the operational independence of Azure China. Consequently, certain services available globally may be unavailable, limited, or modified in Azure China.

Azure China operates under a distinct model compared to its global counterpart, primarily due to the involvement of local partners and regulatory requirements. While Microsoft endeavors to bridge the service availability gap, differences persist. For instance, services like Azure Container Apps and Azure Managed Grafana are not supported in Azure China. Additionally, features such as Azure Monitor integration are unavailable for certain services within the region. These limitations necessitate careful planning and consideration when designing solutions intended for deployment in China.

In practice, these service disparities can pose challenges for organizations aiming to maintain consistency across global and China-based deployments. For example, a company utilizing Azure Event Grid for event-driven architectures globally may need to explore alternative messaging solutions within Azure China due to its unavailability. Similarly, the absence of Azure Monitor container insights requires organizations to implement custom monitoring solutions or leverage third-party tools to achieve comparable observability.

To mitigate these challenges, organizations can adopt several strategies:

- Alternative Services: Identify and utilize alternative Azure services or third-party solutions that offer similar functionality to the unavailable services.
- Custom Implementations: Develop custom solutions to replicate the desired functionalities, ensuring compliance with China's regulatory requirements.
- Hybrid Architectures: Design hybrid architectures that combine Azure China services with on-premises or other cloud providers' offerings to fulfill specific requirements.

- Consultation with Local Partners: Engage with local Azure partners or consultants who possess in-depth knowledge of the Azure China landscape to navigate service limitations effectively.

Given the dynamic nature of cloud service offerings, it's essential to stay informed about the latest developments in Azure China's service availability. Microsoft provides up-to-date documentation detailing the services available in Azure China, which can be accessed here: https://learn.microsoft.com/en-us/azure/china/concepts-service-availability. Regularly consulting this resource ensures that organizations can adapt their strategies to align with the evolving Azure China ecosystem.

Lesson 5

Billing Differences

For organizations expanding into China, one of the most important areas to understand is billing. Azure China, operated independently by 21Vianet, follows a different billing model than global Azure. These differences extend far beyond currency—they affect account structure, purchasing options, payment terms, invoicing, and support contracts. Failing to account for these nuances can lead to budgeting errors, operational delays, and misaligned procurement strategies.

Unlike Azure Global, where users can quickly sign up online and begin consuming services on a pay-as-you-go basis, Azure China offers multiple purchasing models, all of which must comply with local financial regulations. Businesses operating in China must navigate a more controlled and formalized onboarding and billing process.

Azure China currently offers two main purchasing models:

1. Online Services Premium Agreement (OSPA): This is a traditional 3-year enterprise contract where customers can purchase directly from 21Vianet or indirectly via a partner. If purchasing through a partner, the customer signs a commercial agreement with the partner, while maintaining an OSPA with 21Vianet to access and use Azure China services. All support is still provided by 21Vianet, regardless of whether the sale is direct or indirect.

2. 21Vianet Customer Agreement – Enterprise (21VCA-E): This newer and simplified model offers a single, evergreen agreement covering multiple services, reducing the need for multiple contract renewals. It supports both pay-as-you-go (monthly billing) and prepaid options. It comes with integrated cost management, streamlined provisioning, and access to a broader set of services through a unified Azure experience. The minimum annual commitment starts at 1,000 RMB, and billing is conducted entirely in Chinese Yuan (CNY).

All transactions in Azure China are processed in Chinese Yuan (RMB). Invoices are issued by 21Vianet in accordance with local taxation laws and include issuance of fapiao, China's official value-added tax invoice. International payment methods such as credit cards are not accepted. Customers typically settle balances via bank transfer to 21Vianet.

Furthermore, Azure China uses a localized version of the Azure Cost Management portal, tailored to reflect Chinese currency, pricing, and payment terms. However, the billing APIs and UI mirror the global experience for consistency.

Additionally, Azure subscriptions cannot be transferred between Azure China and Azure Global accounts. Each operates in a completely isolated environment, meaning budgets, usage reports, and billing agreements are not interchangeable. Organizations operating in both environments must manage each subscription independently, including invoicing and cost optimization.

Lesson 6

Connectivity Challenges

Connectivity challenges in Azure China are multifaceted, affecting both the performance and reliability of cloud services. Given the unique regulatory environment and infrastructure limitations in the region, IT professionals must navigate a complex landscape. One of the primary issues is the Great Firewall, which imposes restrictions on data flow to and from the global internet. This firewall can cause latency and packet loss, significantly impacting the performance of cloud applications hosted in Azure China. For businesses relying on real-time data processing or global collaboration, these connectivity hurdles can hinder operational efficiency and user experience.

In addition to regulatory barriers, the physical infrastructure supporting internet connectivity in China presents its own set of challenges. Network congestion, especially during peak usage times, can lead to slower response times and service interruptions. Many regions in China still experience limited broadband access, which can restrict the ability of businesses and remote workers to utilize cloud services effectively. Organizations must assess their connectivity options carefully and consider deploying services in multiple regions within China to mitigate these issues and ensure consistent access for users.

Another significant challenge is the integration of Azure China with global Azure services. The separate cloud environments, due to compliance regulations, can complicate hybrid cloud strategies. Businesses that operate both domestically and internationally may find it difficult to synchronize data and applications across these disparate environments. This division necessitates careful planning and architecture design, ensuring that applications can operate seamlessly across both platforms without compromising data integrity or compliance.

To address these challenges, businesses can leverage various strategies. Establishing direct connections through dedicated lines or using Azure ExpressRoute can provide more reliable and faster access to the cloud. Moreover, utilizing Content Delivery Networks (CDNs) can help mitigate latency issues by caching content closer to end-users.

IT professionals should also remain informed about the evolving regulatory landscape and infrastructure developments in China, as this knowledge can inform better decision-making and strategic planning.

In conclusion, while connectivity challenges in Azure China pose significant barriers, understanding these issues allows organizations to devise effective strategies to overcome them. By investing in the right infrastructure, leveraging Azure's capabilities, and staying compliant with local regulations, IT professionals, cloud specialists, and business leaders can successfully navigate the complexities of operating in this unique environment. Embracing these challenges as opportunities for innovation can ultimately lead to enhanced performance and competitive advantage in the rapidly evolving cloud landscape.

Lesson 7

Compliance and Legal Considerations

Compliance and legal considerations are paramount when operating within Azure China, primarily due to the unique regulatory landscape that governs the region. The Chinese government enforces strict data sovereignty laws, which dictate that data pertaining to Chinese citizens and businesses must be stored within the country. IT professionals and cloud service providers must navigate these regulations to ensure compliance, which can involve significant adjustments to data management practices. Understanding the implications of the Cybersecurity Law, the Data Security Law, and the Personal Information Protection Law is essential for any organization looking to leverage Azure services within China.

Organizations utilizing Azure China must also be aware of the licensing requirements and the role of local partnerships. Microsoft has established a joint venture with a local Chinese partner to operate its cloud services, which means that compliance with both local laws and international standards is crucial. This partnership introduces a layer of complexity, as businesses must ensure that their use of Azure aligns with the operational standards set forth by both Microsoft and the Chinese government. IT professionals should engage with legal experts to interpret how these regulations impact their specific use cases and to develop strategies for compliance.

Data privacy is another critical aspect of compliance in Azure China. The Personal Information Protection Law sets stringent guidelines on how personal data can be collected, processed, and stored. Organizations must implement robust data governance frameworks that not only comply with these laws but also build consumer trust. This includes ensuring that data processing agreements are in place and that individuals are informed about how their data will be used. IT professionals should prioritize transparency and user consent in their data handling practices to avoid potential legal repercussions.

Moreover, businesses must consider the implications of cybersecurity measures mandated by Chinese law. The Cybersecurity Law requires organizations to conduct regular security assessments and to implement specific technical measures to protect data.

For companies operating in Azure China, this means that they must ensure their cloud configurations adhere to these requirements. Regular audits and compliance checks should be integrated into the operational processes to identify potential vulnerabilities and to ensure that security protocols are up to date.

Finally, ongoing education and training for employees on compliance issues are essential. As laws and regulations evolve, staying informed is crucial for mitigating risks associated with non-compliance. Organizations should invest in training programs that focus on the legal landscape surrounding cloud operations in China and best practices for data management within Azure. By fostering a culture of compliance and accountability, businesses can better navigate the complexities of operating in Azure China, ultimately leading to more secure and successful cloud deployments.

CHAPTER 3
NAVIGATING THE AZURE CHINA ECOSYSTEM

Lesson 1

Azure Marketplace in China

The Azure Marketplace in China (https://market.azure.cn/) serves as a vital platform for organizations looking to leverage cloud technologies within the region. It offers a unique ecosystem tailored to meet the demands of Chinese enterprises, startups, and IT professionals. This marketplace provides a comprehensive catalog of applications, services, and solutions that are pre-configured to run on Azure's infrastructure. It allows users to discover, purchase, and deploy software and services that enhance their cloud experience while ensuring compliance with local regulations.

One of the key features of the Azure Marketplace in China is its focus on local needs and requirements. The marketplace includes a variety of offerings from both global and local partners, ensuring that businesses can find solutions that align with their specific operational and regulatory frameworks. This localized approach not only enhances the user experience but also accelerates the adoption of cloud technologies among Chinese organizations. By providing tailored solutions, the marketplace supports businesses in overcoming challenges unique to the Chinese market.

Additionally, the Azure Marketplace facilitates seamless integration with existing Azure services. IT professionals can easily deploy applications and services with a few clicks, streamlining workflows and improving efficiency. This integration is particularly beneficial for enterprises looking to scale their operations rapidly while maintaining the flexibility to customize their cloud environments. The ease of use and accessibility of the marketplace empowers businesses to innovate and respond to market demands swiftly.

Security and compliance are paramount in the Azure Marketplace in China. All offerings are rigorously vetted to ensure they meet stringent local regulatory requirements. This focus on security provides peace of mind for businesses concerned about data protection and compliance issues. The marketplace also includes resources that help organizations understand their responsibilities under Chinese law, making it easier for them to navigate the complex regulatory landscape surrounding cloud services.

Ultimately, the Azure Marketplace in China represents a significant opportunity for businesses of all sizes to harness the power of cloud computing. By leveraging the diverse array of solutions available, organizations can drive digital transformation, improve operational efficiency, and foster innovation. As more enterprises recognize the strategic advantages of utilizing Azure's capabilities within China, the marketplace will play an increasingly important role in shaping the future of cloud adoption in the region.

Lesson 2

Azure China ExpressRoute and Networking Solutions

Establishing a secure, high-performance, and compliant network infrastructure is fundamental for organizations deploying services in Azure China. Unlike Azure's global footprint, Azure China is operated independently by 21Vianet and governed by Chinese regulatory requirements. This operational separation affects not only how services are accessed but also how networking and connectivity are designed and implemented. Among the most critical components in this environment are ExpressRoute, VPN Gateway, Azure China's localized CDN offering, and hybrid integration models that enable multi-region or cross-border operations.

Azure China ExpressRoute is a dedicated, private network connection that links a customer's on-premises infrastructure directly to Microsoft Azure China data centers. It bypasses the public internet entirely, offering more consistent throughput, lower latency, and enhanced security features that are essential for mission-critical applications and sensitive data operations. Organizations can choose from multiple connectivity models such as point-to-point Ethernet connections or MPLS VPNs offered through approved Chinese telecom providers. Bandwidth options are flexible and scalable, allowing businesses to adapt their network capacity as demand increases. ExpressRoute circuits are also available between region pairs within China. For example, there are free circuits between China North and China North 2, or China East and China East 2. These circuits support seamless replication and high availability across regions with minimal latency, critical for disaster recovery and geo-redundant deployments.

For businesses that need secure connectivity but do not require the performance and reliability of dedicated ExpressRoute circuits, Azure China also supports Azure VPN Gateway. This allows encrypted connections over the public internet between on-premises networks and Azure China, supporting both site-to-site and point-to-site VPN configurations. While VPN-based connections are more economical and easier to deploy than ExpressRoute, they are better suited to development environments or less latency-sensitive workloads.

In addition to direct connectivity, delivering content quickly and reliably to end users within China remains a persistent challenge due to the country's controlled internet infrastructure. To address this, Azure China offers a localized Content Delivery Network (CDN), which leverages partnerships with regional CDN providers such as ChinaCache or Wangsu. This allows businesses to serve static and dynamic content from points of presence (PoPs) distributed throughout China. The Azure China CDN intelligently selects the optimal provider based on geographic proximity and performance. However, to use CDN services within China, organizations must obtain an Internet Content Provider (ICP) license, a legal requirement for hosting any public-facing content in the country. It's also worth noting that Azure China's CDN offering is entirely separate from Azure Global's CDN services and requires a dedicated Azure China subscription.

As cloud strategies evolve, many international companies face the challenge of managing environments both inside and outside China. Because Azure China is completely isolated from Azure Global, cross-border integration requires careful design. Hybrid networking solutions are often the answer. For example, some enterprises operate dual ExpressRoute circuits, one in Azure Global and one in Azure China and use on-premises infrastructure as a communication bridge. Others implement VPN tunnels that connect an international data center to both Azure environments. These architectures allow partial integration while maintaining regulatory compliance, but they also introduce complexity in areas like identity management, directory synchronization, and data flow control.

To ease some of this complexity, Microsoft and its telecom partners in China offer a bundled solution known as the "China Express Model." This approach provides end-to-end networking support, including ExpressRoute provisioning, infrastructure guidance, and regulatory compliance assistance, all under a single contract. It helps simplify what can otherwise be a time-consuming and bureaucratic process.

Security remains a central concern in all Azure China networking operations. ExpressRoute, by avoiding public internet routes, greatly reduces exposure to external threats. VPNs use encrypted tunnels to secure traffic in transit. Furthermore, tools such as Azure Network Security Groups (NSGs), Application Security Groups (ASGs), and Azure Firewall are available to create defense-in-depth strategies. Azure China supports these services to ensure enterprises meet the same internal governance and compliance objectives they maintain globally.

Ultimately, building and managing networking in Azure China is not merely a technical task; it is a strategic endeavor that must align with local laws, infrastructure realities, and business performance goals. Whether deploying a hybrid architecture, implementing a local CDN, or provisioning a private ExpressRoute circuit, organizations must architect their networks with both compliance and performance in mind. These decisions often determine the success of a cloud deployment and the experience delivered to customers within China's tightly controlled digital ecosystem.

Lesson 3

Pricing Tools and Cost Management in Azure China

Pricing tools and cost management are essential components for effectively utilizing Azure China, given the unique market dynamics and regulatory environment. Azure China offers a variety of pricing models that cater to different business needs. Understanding these models allows organizations to choose the most cost-effective options for their cloud services. From pay-as-you-go to reserved instances, Azure China provides flexibility in pricing that can help businesses optimize their cloud spending based on usage patterns and workloads.

One of the key tools available in Azure China for cost management is the Azure Pricing Calculator (https://www.azure.cn/pricing/calculator/). This tool enables users to estimate the costs associated with various Azure services by inputting specific configurations and expected usage levels. The pricing calculator helps businesses project their monthly expenses, making it easier to budget and allocate resources effectively. By providing a detailed breakdown of costs, organizations can assess the financial impact of their cloud architecture choices and identify potential areas for cost savings.

In addition to the pricing calculator, Azure China offers Azure Cost Management, which provides insights into cloud spending and usage. This tool allows organizations to monitor their Azure consumption in real time, helping them understand where their resources are being allocated. With features such as cost analysis, budgeting, and forecasting, companies can make informed decisions about their cloud investments. The ability to set spending alerts and thresholds further empowers organizations to maintain control over their budgets, reducing the risk of unexpected expenses.

Moreover, Azure China supports advanced cost management strategies through the use of tags and resource groups. By tagging resources according to department, project, or environment, businesses can gain better visibility into their spending patterns. This level of granularity enables organizations to identify which areas of their operations are incurring higher costs and adjust their strategies accordingly.

Resource grouping also simplifies the management of costs by consolidating related resources, making it easier to analyze and optimize overall expenditures.

Finally, regular reviews of pricing and cost management strategies are crucial for maintaining efficiency in Azure China. As cloud services evolve, so too do pricing models and available discounts. Organizations should stay informed about changes in Azure pricing, promotional offers, and new service options that may impact their cost structure. By adopting a proactive approach to cost management, businesses can ensure that they are not only effectively utilizing Azure China's pricing tools but also aligning their cloud strategy with their overall financial goals.

Lesson 4

Microsoft Partner Network (MPN) in China

The Microsoft Partner Network (MPN) in China serves as a critical framework for organizations looking to leverage Microsoft's cloud solutions, particularly Azure. This partnership program provides a comprehensive set of resources, tools, and support to help companies build, sell, and service their cloud-based offerings. With China's rapid digital transformation and increasing demand for cloud services, MPN opens doors for IT professionals, cloud specialists, and business leaders to enhance their capabilities and better serve their clients in this dynamic market.

One of the primary benefits of joining the MPN in China is access to a vast range of resources tailored to local needs. Partners gain exclusive access to training programs, technical support, and marketing assets that can help them navigate the unique challenges of the Chinese market. These resources empower businesses to improve their technical skills in Azure, develop innovative solutions, and effectively reach potential customers. The MPN also facilitates networking opportunities, allowing partners to connect with other businesses, industry experts, and Microsoft representatives, fostering collaboration and knowledge sharing.

MPN members can choose from various partnership levels, including the Silver and Gold competencies. Each level provides distinct advantages, such as enhanced technical support and eligibility for exclusive incentives. For companies focused on specific areas like application development, data analytics, or cloud infrastructure, achieving a Gold competency can significantly elevate their market position. It demonstrates a commitment to excellence and assures clients of their expertise, which is particularly important in a competitive landscape like China's cloud services market.

The MPN also plays a vital role in compliance and regulatory adherence, which is essential for businesses operating in China. With stringent regulations governing data privacy and security, Microsoft partners receive guidance on aligning their solutions with local laws and industry standards.

This support not only helps organizations mitigate risks but also enhances their credibility with clients who prioritize compliance. By leveraging MPN resources, partners can confidently navigate the complexities of operating within China's regulatory environment.

Finally, the MPN in China fosters a culture of innovation among its partners. Microsoft encourages collaboration on new solutions that address local market needs, thereby driving technological advancement. This focus on innovation not only benefits individual businesses but also contributes to the overall growth of the cloud ecosystem in China. By tapping into the resources and community provided by MPN, IT professionals and business leaders can position themselves at the forefront of cloud technology, ultimately leading to increased competitiveness and success in the marketplace.

Lesson 5

Azure China Support Plans

Navigating support in Azure China requires an understanding that differs significantly from the global Azure experience. In China, Microsoft Azure is operated by 21Vianet, and as such, all support plans and customer service models are managed locally under this partnership. This structure ensures compliance with local regulations while offering tailored assistance to enterprises, developers, and government entities deploying solutions on Azure within China's borders.

21Vianet offers multiple tiers of Azure support services to accommodate the varying needs of its customers. For small teams working on test or proof-of-concept environments, the Developer Support Plan is often the preferred entry point. It provides guidance during development, with access to technical support during business hours. For customers managing production workloads where uptime and responsiveness are critical, the Standard Support Plan introduces 24/7 access for high-severity issues, allowing for more robust operational support. At the enterprise level, large organizations benefit from the Enterprise Support Plan, often referred to as Unified Support which includes proactive architectural guidance, a designated Customer Success Account Manager (CSAM), and faster response times across the board.

Access to support is facilitated through several channels that are adapted to China's digital ecosystem. Customers can submit tickets via the 21Vianet online portal or the Services Hub, depending on their contract type. For urgent technical issues, 24/7 phone support is available via two official hotlines: +86 800-820-1859 for landline users and +86 400-820-1859 for mobile calls. In addition, recognizing the prevalence of mobile messaging platforms in China, 21Vianet also provides WeChat-based support through their official support handle, VNET_AzureSupport. This WeChat channel is particularly useful for follow-ups, quick troubleshooting guidance, and service notifications. Response times vary depending on the severity of the issue and the selected plan. For example, a Severity A incident under the Enterprise plan receives an initial response within one hour, ensuring that business-critical applications and services get prioritized attention.

Lower severity levels and Developer-tier incidents receive responses aligned with their operational expectations, generally during working hours. This structure reflects a localized approach while preserving the principles of Microsoft's global support framework.

Billing and contractual agreements for Azure support services in China are entirely managed by 21Vianet and follow Chinese financial laws. All payments are processed in Chinese Yuan (CNY), and official invoices (fapiaos) are issued in compliance with domestic tax standards. As with all aspects of Azure China operations, these localized practices reflect the broader theme of sovereign cloud control ensuring data, contracts, and service delivery stay within China's jurisdiction.

CHAPTER 4
COMPLIANCE AND SECURITY FOR AZURE IN CHINA

Lesson 1

Overview of Regulatory Requirements

The regulatory landscape in China is characterized by a complex interplay of laws and policies that govern the use of cloud services, particularly in the context of Azure. IT professionals and business leaders must navigate a maze of regulations that dictate how data can be stored, processed, and transferred. Key regulations include the Cybersecurity Law, the Data Security Law, and the Personal Information Protection Law, each imposing stringent requirements on organizations operating in the cloud. Understanding these laws is critical for compliance and to mitigate risks associated with data breaches and non-compliance penalties.

One of the central tenets of the regulatory framework is the requirement for data localization. Organizations must ensure that data pertaining to Chinese citizens is stored within the country's borders. This requirement directly impacts cloud architecture and necessitates the use of local data centers. Azure China, operated by 21Vianet, complies with these regulations by providing services from local data centers, ensuring that organizations can meet their legal obligations while leveraging cloud technology. IT professionals must therefore design their infrastructure with these restrictions in mind to avoid potential legal repercussions.

In addition to data localization, the regulations emphasize the importance of data security measures. Organizations are required to implement robust cybersecurity practices to protect sensitive information from unauthorized access and breaches. This includes conducting regular security assessments, implementing encryption, and establishing incident response protocols. Azure China offers various tools and services that assist organizations in meeting these security standards, but the ultimate responsibility lies with the businesses themselves. IT and cloud professionals must be proactive in integrating these security measures into their cloud strategy. Furthermore, companies must be aware of the implications of cross-border data transfers. While certain data may be allowed to leave the country, it often requires specific permissions and adherence to stringent conditions.

The regulatory framework outlines clear guidelines on obtaining consent for data transfer, ensuring that organizations remain compliant when operating in a global environment. Business leaders must understand these nuances to navigate international operations successfully, as non-compliance can lead to significant fines and operational disruptions.

Lastly, the regulatory environment is continually evolving, and organizations must stay informed about upcoming changes. New policies and amendments to existing laws can impact how cloud services are utilized and governed. Continuous education and awareness of regulatory updates are essential for IT professionals and business leaders alike. Engaging with legal experts and participating in industry forums can provide valuable insights and help organizations adapt to regulatory changes effectively. By staying ahead of the curve, businesses can leverage Azure China's offerings while ensuring compliance and fostering trust with their customers.

Lesson 2

Azure Shared Responsibility Model in China

The Azure Shared Responsibility Model in China is a crucial framework that delineates the security and compliance obligations between Microsoft and its customers. In the context of Azure services, this model clarifies the division of responsibilities, ensuring that both Microsoft and the users understand their roles in maintaining the security and integrity of data stored in the cloud. This model is particularly significant in China, where regulatory requirements and data sovereignty issues necessitate a more nuanced approach to cloud security.

Under the Shared Responsibility Model, Microsoft is responsible for the security of the cloud infrastructure itself, which includes physical security, network controls, and the security of the virtualization layer. This encompasses the data centers and the hardware that support Azure services. In China, where strict regulations govern data protection and privacy, Microsoft ensures compliance with local laws, providing assurance that the infrastructure is secure and continuously monitored against threats. Understanding this layer of responsibility is essential for businesses operating in China, as it sets the foundation for a secure cloud environment.

On the other hand, customers are responsible for securing their applications, data, and identities within the Azure environment. This includes configuring security settings, managing access controls, and ensuring that sensitive data is encrypted. In China, where businesses must navigate complex regulatory landscapes, it is vital for organizations to implement robust security policies and practices to protect their assets. The emphasis on customer responsibility highlights the need for IT professionals to be well-versed in Azure security features and best practices to mitigate risks effectively.

Moreover, the Shared Responsibility Model in China emphasizes the importance of compliance with national regulations, such as the Cybersecurity Law and the Personal Information Protection Law. Organizations must be proactive in understanding these regulations and how they intersect with their use of Azure services.

Microsoft provides various compliance certifications and documentation that can assist businesses in aligning their cloud practices with local laws. However, it remains the responsibility of the organizations to ensure that their cloud deployments comply with these regulations.

In conclusion, the Azure Shared Responsibility Model in China serves as a foundational guideline for organizations leveraging cloud services. By clearly defining the roles of both Microsoft and its customers, this model enhances the security posture of businesses and fosters a culture of accountability. IT and cloud professionals, alongside business leaders, must engage with this model to ensure comprehensive security strategies are in place, thereby enabling their organizations to thrive in the dynamic and regulated cloud landscape of China.

Lesson 3

Data Security and Government Access in Azure China

In Azure China, security is not only a technical requirement it is a foundational expectation shaped by regulatory, operational, and geopolitical realities. Operated by 21Vianet under a sovereign cloud model, Azure China enforces distinct security standards to align with the Chinese government's data protection laws, including the Cybersecurity Law, Data Security Law, and Personal Information Protection Law (PIPL). These frameworks place strict mandates on how data is stored, accessed, and protected, and influence how foreign and domestic organizations deploy cloud workloads within the country.

At the core of Azure China's security model lies Microsoft's global security architecture, which is licensed and implemented by 21Vianet. Despite operating independently, Azure China maintains the same shared responsibility model as global Azure where Microsoft is responsible for securing the infrastructure, and the customer is responsible for securing their data, identity, and applications. However, security implementations in China must also factor in local compliance auditing, government oversight, and potential data disclosure obligations, especially for regulated industries such as finance, telecom, and healthcare.

A frequent question from international customers is whether 21Vianet or government agencies can access their data. Officially, 21Vianet does not access customer data unless it is required to maintain the service or compelled by Chinese law or a formal regulatory request. This mirrors how global Microsoft services function in other jurisdictions with compliance obligations. That said, businesses operating in China should be prepared for greater scrutiny and a higher likelihood of receiving regulatory inquiries or audits, particularly when handling large datasets, cross-border transfers, or sensitive information.

To address these concerns, Azure China provides enterprise-grade security controls similar to those available globally. Features such as Azure Active Directory, Network Security Groups, Azure Key Vault, and Azure Firewall are available and should be implemented from the outset. Role-based access control (RBAC) should be tightly enforced, with multi-factor authentication (MFA) enabled for all users.

Encryption both at rest and in transit should be configured using customer-managed keys wherever possible, giving businesses tighter control over data security in the event of audit or investigation.

Because Chinese law allows for potential government data access, especially when public safety or national security is cited, companies must also evaluate legal risk exposure. This includes reviewing their data classification practices, access policies, and compliance reporting workflows. Engaging legal counsel with expertise in Chinese cybersecurity regulations is not only recommended but often essential for building a compliant and defensible cloud governance strategy.

Lesson 4

Data Residency in Azure China

Data residency in Azure China is a non-negotiable compliance pillar and one of the first factors every business must consider when migrating workloads into the Chinese market. Unlike global Azure, which offers data residency options by region, Azure China is a fully isolated instance of the Microsoft cloud. Operated by 21Vianet, it ensures that all data, whether in storage, transit, or processing, remains within China's borders, in accordance with national data sovereignty regulations.

Chinese laws, especially the Data Security Law (DSL) and the Personal Information Protection Law (PIPL), stipulate that data collected within China must be stored and managed locally, and certain categories of data such as critical information infrastructure (CII) or personal data must not be transferred outside China without explicit government review and approval. Azure China was architected to meet these requirements, offering customers a compliant platform where data localization is enforced at the infrastructure level.

From a practical standpoint, this means that Azure services hosted in Azure Global are not interoperable with Azure China services. Applications, backups, databases, and API calls must be fully contained within Azure China's environment. There is no direct peering, integration, or federation between global and China regions. This often requires businesses to maintain duplicate environments one for global operations and one for Chinese users raising operational complexity, deployment overhead, and additional costs.

Organizations that assume "lift and shift" strategies can seamlessly apply from global Azure often encounter limitations. Services available in global Azure may be missing or offered with different feature sets in China, which can impact architecture decisions. Moreover, enterprises must monitor and validate that no metadata or logging information is inadvertently routed to services hosted outside of China for instance, using global endpoints instead of China-specific ones when configuring SDKs or APIs. A real-world example involves a global e-commerce client that used a global Azure CDN for media asset delivery.

After expanding into China, they had to reconfigure their entire CDN architecture to use Azure China's localized CDN and ensure compliance with the ICP licensing process for public web content. Even services as basic as Azure Monitor or Azure Policy had to be re-evaluated, as telemetry and logging endpoints defaulted to global configurations unless explicitly overridden.

To maintain proper data residency, IT leaders must audit their infrastructure routinely and ensure all services and dependencies are mapped to the Azure China region. Where necessary, businesses should opt for Azure Resource Graph, Azure Cost Management, and custom tagging policies to track and visualize the geographical residency of their workloads. Azure China's compliance documentation, maintained by 21Vianet, provides a clear outline of which services are offered and how they handle data.

CHAPTER 5

MASTERING AZURE CHINA SERVICES

Lesson 1

Azure Services in China

Understanding Azure China's service landscape is essential for anyone planning to build, scale, or operate cloud-native applications within mainland China. While Microsoft Azure's global platform offers a consistent experience across regions, Azure China—operated by 21Vianet—is unique in both its regulatory framework and service availability. Services must not only meet technical demands but also align with China's strict data residency laws, government approvals, and isolated infrastructure. Therefore, success begins with knowing which services are available, how they differ from their global counterparts, and how to design around these constraints.

As of 2024, Azure China provides over 100 core services, but not all Azure Global offerings are available in the China regions. Services often launch months—or even years—after they debut globally, and some are significantly modified to meet regulatory compliance. For example, services that rely on data transfers across regions or depend on U.S.-hosted infrastructure may be delayed or unavailable. The Azure China Service Availability page (https://learn.microsoft.com/en-us/azure/china/concepts-service-availability) should be every IT leader's first stop when architecting solutions in this market.

Among the most widely used and reliable services is Azure Virtual Machines (VMs). Azure China supports a range of VM sizes, series, and OS images, including Windows Server, Ubuntu, Red Hat, and CentOS. Local enterprises in sectors like manufacturing and finance often deploy hybrid workloads that require specific VM configurations and must comply with Multi-Level Protection Scheme (MLPS) 2.0 requirements. Azure VMs support managed disks, custom images, availability sets, and virtual scale sets, though users must double-check which disk types and regions support each capability. For example, premium SSDs are not yet available in all zones across China North 3 or China East 2. Web application development is equally robust through Azure App Service, which allows rapid deployment of .NET, Java, Node.js, Python, and PHP-based applications. Startups and SaaS companies entering China often use App Service to launch lightweight portals and admin dashboards.

One U.S.-based edtech firm used Azure App Service in China East to host its mobile app backend for its Chinese users, integrating seamlessly with Azure CDN (China) and Azure Application Gateway to boost performance and comply with ICP licensing rules.

For cloud-native developers, Azure Kubernetes Service (AKS) is now available in Azure China, albeit with some feature limitations compared to global regions. While AKS in China supports autoscaling and integrated monitoring via Azure Monitor, some container governance features like Azure Defender for Kubernetes may be delayed in availability. DevOps teams often use Azure Container Registry (ACR) alongside AKS to maintain image pipelines entirely within China's digital borders, which is crucial for compliance and latency optimization.

Data platforms are another pillar of Azure China's offering. Azure SQL Database, a fully managed relational database-as-a-service, is used by thousands of enterprises across China. It supports zone-redundant deployments, elastic pools, and built-in threat detection, enabling highly available transactional workloads. For globally scaled architectures, businesses often mirror Azure SQL in China alongside SQL in Europe or the U.S., synchronizing anonymized or aggregated data manually to avoid cross-border legal complications.

For distributed NoSQL workloads, Azure Cosmos DB offers multi-model support with tunable consistency levels ideal for mobile backends, recommendation engines, or gaming platforms. That said, Cosmos DB availability in Azure China can vary by API. For example, the MongoDB API is supported, but Gremlin and Cassandra support may be limited or pending. Enterprises must test Cosmos DB service quotas regionally, as throughput configurations (RU/s) may differ compared to Azure Global.

Advanced analytics and BI workloads are well-supported through Azure Synapse Analytics and Azure Data Factory, both available in Azure China. These tools empower enterprises to ingest, transform, and visualize massive datasets—often from IoT sensors, ERP platforms, or ecommerce streams without compromising on performance or compliance. One multinational electronics firm deployed Azure Synapse in China North 3 to run product failure analysis using historical sensor data. They built a localized Power BI dashboard (using Power BI China service) that gave regional managers visibility without exporting any raw data outside China's borders.

From a security and identity standpoint, Azure Security Center, Azure Key Vault, and Azure Active Directory (AAD) form the backbone of governance and compliance. AAD in Azure China supports SSO, conditional access policies, and integration with Microsoft 365 China services, though cross-tenant and B2B integrations are often more restricted than global Azure.

Azure China also provides local versions of Cost Management, Azure Monitor, and Azure Policy, which allow teams to maintain operational efficiency and budget control. One retail company reduced its monthly compute bill by over 25% by applying Advisor recommendations, right-sizing VMs, and setting budgets via Cost Management dashboards in Chinese yuan (RMB).

Lesson 2

Service Gaps in Azure China

While Azure China has matured significantly since its launch in 2014, it still operates under a sovereign model that introduces important constraints when compared to Azure Global. These differences are driven not only by technical limitations but by China's complex regulatory framework, operational approvals, and data sovereignty policies. For IT professionals, cloud architects, and business decision-makers, understanding which Azure services are missing, delayed, or restricted in China is critical to avoid roadblocks and design compliant, resilient cloud architectures.

One of the most noticeable gaps lies in artificial intelligence and machine learning services. While Azure Machine Learning, Cognitive Services, and Bot Services are available in select regions of Azure China, they often lack full feature parity with their global counterparts. For instance, some pre-trained language models used for text analysis or image recognition— available globally are unavailable or restricted in China due to content regulation and model compliance constraints. A global financial services firm, for example, had to re-train its global fraud detection model locally using open-source tools because the built-in anomaly detection model in Azure ML was not accessible in China. For teams reliant on global AI APIs (e.g., translation, facial recognition, voice services), hybrid architectures or local open-source model hosting often become the only feasible solution.

Another significant limitation is in the data analytics and big data ecosystem. While Azure Synapse Analytics is technically available in China, it frequently lacks advanced integration capabilities with services such as Azure Data Lake Storage Gen2, Azure Purview, and Power BI Embedded, which are tightly integrated in global deployments. Additionally, serverless SQL pool and Apache Spark pools, key components for scalable and interactive analytics, may either be unavailable or lag significantly in performance due to backend isolation. Organizations with heavy data science and warehousing needs often resort to building pipelines with Azure Data Factory, writing to SQL Database or Blob Storage, and analyzing with localized BI tools like FineBI or Yonghong BI. It's a more fragmented experience, but it ensures compliance with China's cybersecurity and data localization laws.

DevOps and developer tooling also face notable constraints. While Azure DevOps is accessible in China, the experience is degraded due to restricted integrations with external tools, limited Marketplace availability, and occasionally slower Git clone/push operations due to infrastructure throttling. Furthermore, services such as GitHub Actions, Visual Studio Code remote extensions, and GitHub Copilot are not natively integrated with Azure China accounts, which affects CI/CD pipelines for development teams that depend on a tightly coupled DevOps toolchain. As a workaround, companies often host self-managed agents for Azure Pipelines and use private Git repositories or Gitee (a GitHub alternative widely used in China) for source control.

Security and compliance services in Azure China, although aligned with Chinese standards, often lag behind in terms of automated governance, security recommendations, and integrations with Microsoft Defender for Cloud. While Azure Security Center exists in Azure China, certain features like automatic policy enforcement across multi-subscription environments or integrations with Microsoft Sentinel may not be available or require manual setup. For companies with complex compliance obligations (e.g., financial services, life sciences, or automotive sectors), this creates a heavier operational burden. Many organizations have had to implement custom security auditing scripts using Azure Monitor logs and manual compliance frameworks tailored to local requirements such as MLPS 2.0 and classified information protection standards.

A frequently overlooked area is the availability of new releases and preview services. Azure China often trails Azure Global by 12–18 months in launching new capabilities. For example, Azure OpenAI Service, which enables integration with powerful GPT-based models, is not available in Azure China as of 2024 due to regulatory concerns over large language models and content generation. This means teams looking to implement conversational AI or natural language interfaces must build and train local models using platforms like Baidu PaddlePaddle, Tencent Cloud's AI toolkit, or deploy fine-tuned open-source models within Azure VMs or containers.

Other missing or limited services include:

- Azure Arc-enabled services (e.g., Arc-enabled SQL Server, Arc for Kubernetes) – partially available.
- Azure Quantum, Azure Percept, Azure Maps, and Mixed Reality Services – currently unavailable.
- Azure Event Grid often limited to basic use cases and not supported in all China regions.
- Azure Media Services may lack support for live streaming or DRM due to content approval restrictions.

These service gaps affect not only feature availability but also how you plan your architecture and rollout strategy. It is not uncommon for global companies to maintain dual deployment strategies, one for Azure Global and one for Azure China connected only through air-gapped environments, VPNs, or localized API interfaces. One European consumer electronics company, for instance, developed its AI video analysis pipeline globally but deployed only the inference models inside China on GPU-powered Azure VMs, with user interface integration managed through Azure App Service in China East 2.

Lesson 3

Best Practices for Optimizing Azure China Services

Optimizing Azure China services goes far beyond routine performance tuning it demands a strategy that is mindful of regulatory constraints, regional service limitations, infrastructure isolation, and cost visibility. For IT professionals, cloud architects, and business leaders, getting the most out of Azure China requires a hybrid of technical precision, localized best practices, and an understanding of the market's operational realities. Whether you're managing a hybrid cloud architecture, a high-traffic e-commerce platform, or a SaaS workload, the optimization playbook in Azure China starts with awareness and ends with iteration.

One of the first pillars of optimization is compliance-informed architecture. In China, laws such as the Cybersecurity Law, Data Security Law, and Personal Information Protection Law (PIPL) dictate that certain types of data, particularly personal, sensitive, or operational data must remain within China's borders. This affects everything from how your logs are stored to how your disaster recovery plan is architected. Services like Azure Key Vault, Azure SQL, and Azure Monitor must be deployed within mainland China regions (e.g., China North 3 or China East 2). Businesses that fail to adhere to this may face operational disruption or compliance penalties. Using Azure China's Trust Center and engaging legal advisors with MLPS 2.0 experience is a foundational step toward secure optimization.

When it comes to performance tuning, one of the most overlooked factors in Azure China is region selection and latency optimization. Although Azure China is expanding most recently with the China North 3 region in Hebei, some global customers are unaware that Azure China regions cannot interconnect with global Azure. This means that workloads cannot be spread across global and Chinese regions, and CDN nodes or DNS zones need to be deployed specifically for China. For public-facing services, pairing Azure China CDN with Azure Front Door (China version) and Application Gateway can drastically reduce latency. A multinational logistics company saw page load times drop by over 40% after migrating their web content to Azure CDN China and deploying static content in China East 2, aligned with their Shanghai user base.

To optimize infrastructure and deployment workflows, leveraging Azure Resource Manager (ARM) templates, Bicep, or Terraform (China-compatible) can reduce manual errors and enforce consistency. However, developers must adapt templates to region-specific resource types and APIs. Additionally, some global DevOps pipelines must be mirrored or rebuilt within China due to API endpoint differences. One SaaS company overcame Azure DevOps Marketplace limitations by running self-hosted agents inside China and using Git repositories hosted on Gitee, GitHub's Chinese alternative, to support localized build and release automation.

A key component of optimization is monitoring and observability. Tools like Azure Monitor, Log Analytics, and Application Insights are fully supported in Azure China, but they require separate configuration compared to global deployments. IT teams should set up custom dashboards tailored to region-specific telemetry. This includes tracking ingress/egress bandwidth, CPU/IO utilization on premium disks (which are not universally available across all regions), and VM availability zone health. By establishing proactive alert rules, autoscaling policies, and anomaly detection, teams can quickly adapt to traffic surges, infrastructure degradation, or potential cost spikes. Enterprises that implement full monitoring stacks in China often see a 15–25% improvement in mean time to resolution (MTTR) and more predictable scaling outcomes.

From a cost optimization perspective, Azure China presents both challenges and opportunities. Billing is processed in Chinese Yuan (RMB), and the cost calculator for Azure China differs from Azure Global. Pricing for virtual machines, data storage, and bandwidth can vary by region, and certain services like Azure Backup or Azure Site Recovery may not be cost-effective or even available. Smart organizations use Azure Cost Management (China) to set budgets, alerts, and spending targets, segment costs by business units or environments, and implement reserved instances or spot VMs for predictable workloads. A digital agency serving ecommerce platforms reduced their monthly Azure China bill by 31% simply by identifying underutilized VMs and shifting to reserved capacity across three client accounts.

Finally, continuous education and community engagement are essential for staying ahead. Azure China releases new services in a staggered timeline compared to Azure Global sometimes 12–18 months later.

Keeping up with the Azure China blog and official documentation, attending regional Microsoft events, and joining local developer groups (like those on QQ or WeChat) are invaluable for maintaining a future-proof architecture. IT leaders should also encourage engineers to complete region-specific training and certifications through Microsoft Learn China to deepen local cloud fluency.

CHAPTER 6
BUILDING A RESILIENT AZURE CHINA INFRASTRUCTURE

Lesson 1

Architecting for High Availability

High availability (HA) is not just a best practice in cloud architecture it's a fundamental business requirement in the modern digital landscape. In Azure China, where service delivery is governed by a unique operational framework managed by 21Vianet, architecting for HA takes on additional complexity. Businesses operating in China must ensure continuous service uptime despite potential regulatory delays, regional failovers, or infrastructure limitations. This requires careful design, deep understanding of Azure China's architecture, and constant validation.

At its core, high availability refers to the ability of a system or service to remain operational and accessible for a significant portion of time typically defined by SLAs of 99.9%, 99.95%, or higher. For instance, a service with a 99.95% SLA allows for just over 21 minutes of downtime per month. In high-demand industries like e-commerce, finance, and manufacturing common in Azure China, downtime of even a few minutes can translate into major revenue loss and reputational damage.

One of the most effective strategies for achieving HA in Azure China is leveraging Availability Zones, which are physically separated data centers within the same Azure region. Each zone is equipped with independent power, cooling, and networking. Microsoft ensures that no single point of failure in one zone will impact services in another. For example, the newly launched China North 3 region (Hebei) includes three Availability Zones, enabling advanced deployment patterns for resilient architectures. Organizations that distribute their application workloads and data services across multiple zones gain true fault isolation—if one zone goes offline, the others remain functional.

For applications with global components or customer bases spread across provinces, Azure Traffic Manager becomes a crucial service. It enables geo-routing, weighted traffic distribution, and endpoint failover between regions or availability zones. Imagine a multinational firm running a China-based e-commerce storefront hosted in China North 3 with a DR site in China East 2.

With Traffic Manager, the firm can automatically reroute users to the healthy endpoint in case of regional failure, minimizing downtime and maintaining customer experience.

Load balancing at the infrastructure layer is also vital. Azure Load Balancer and Application Gateway provide Layer 4 and Layer 7 distribution, respectively. Azure Load Balancer is often used to distribute traffic across multiple VM instances of the same tier, ensuring continuous service delivery even if a single instance fails. Application Gateway adds features like SSL termination and web application firewall (WAF) integration, which are especially important for public-facing services dealing with volatile traffic patterns or regional attack vectors.

Equally important is monitoring and observability. Azure China offers Azure Monitor, Log Analytics, and Application Insights, giving teams visibility into performance metrics, service health, and user experience. These tools should be configured to track key availability indicators, such as request failure rates, latency spikes, and CPU utilization. Proactive alerting allows operational teams to respond in real-time to emerging incidents, often before end users are impacted. For example, alerts can be set to trigger when a web app's response time exceeds 500 milliseconds in any availability zone, prompting an automated scale-out action.

One of the challenges unique to Azure China is the lag in global feature parity. Not all HA-related services available in global Azure are instantly released in China. For example, services like Zone Redundant Storage (ZRS) or Availability Zone support for specific SKUs may become available later in China than in other regions. Organizations must regularly consult the official Azure China service availability list (https://learn.microsoft.com/en-us/azure/china/concepts-service-availability) to design infrastructure with only available features and avoid deploying architectures reliant on unsupported options.

To mitigate these limitations, many enterprises implement layered redundancy: combining Active-Active deployments across regions with active-passive failover patterns at the application tier. In one case, a logistics provider deployed containerized microservices across China North 3 and China East 1 using Kubernetes (AKS) clusters with synchronized stateful data in Azure SQL and blob storage. A lightweight traffic management layer allowed seamless switching between environments in less than 30 seconds during failovers achieving a practical SLA of 99.98%.

Finally, high availability is not just about setup it's about validation. Organizations must run resilience testing, such as Azure Chaos Studio (where supported) or manual simulated outages to verify that failovers, alerts, and recovery workflows behave as expected. Regular disaster recovery drills, load tests, and performance tuning exercises not only reinforce infrastructure resilience but also build operational confidence within engineering and DevOps teams.

Lesson 2

Networking in China

Building resilient cloud infrastructure in China starts with mastering the complex, sometimes counterintuitive, world of networking in the region. While in global Azure environments network architecture might be mostly a technical challenge, in China it is an intersection of technology, regulation, compliance, performance constraints, and local partnerships. For professionals deploying services in Azure China, networking is often the first and most significant bottleneck to solve.

The technical challenge is not trivial. Internet connectivity between mainland China and the rest of the world is highly restricted and controlled under the so-called "Great Firewall." Latency to global endpoints is unpredictable, bandwidth is limited by the government's licensed telecom carriers, and routing is often asymmetric. This has significant implications for any application requiring multi-region connectivity or integration with systems outside of China. As a result, Azure China is designed to be fully isolated from global Azure environments. There is no direct peering, and even basic services such as DNS resolution or storage access must remain within the Chinese network to comply with data residency laws and avoid latency-related failures.

Microsoft's solution to this challenge is to treat Azure China as a completely sovereign cloud. It is operated by 21Vianet, hosted in data centers physically located in mainland China, and connected to the local backbone networks of China Telecom, China Unicom, and China Mobile. These providers are the only ones licensed to operate cross-province backbone networks, and all traffic internal and external must pass through their infrastructure. To this end, Azure ExpressRoute China becomes the most reliable way to connect enterprise infrastructure to the Azure China cloud. By leveraging a private MPLS or Ethernet connection to one of 21Vianet's data centers, organizations can establish secure, low-latency connections that bypass the unreliable public internet.

These technical solutions, however, must be aligned with compliance considerations. All public-facing applications in China must obtain an ICP license (Internet Content Provider License) issued by the Chinese Ministry of Industry and Information Technology (MIIT).

Without this license, organizations are not allowed to serve websites or APIs hosted within China to end-users. Many organizations have been forced to delay or redesign their deployments due to ICP-related complications, and having local partners or system integrators to navigate the process is invaluable.

Beyond compliance, network design in Azure China must be regionally aware. Azure China currently operates in three main production regions: China East, China North, and China North 3 (Hebei). Not all regions have the same service availability or performance characteristics. For example, China North 3 is the most modern, with three Availability Zones and full ExpressRoute support. Microsoft also offers free ExpressRoute circuits between region pairs like North 1–North 2 or East 1–East 2 to promote disaster recovery architectures. However, some regions like China East 3 are designated as DR-only and are not available for general provisioning.

Due to the isolation between Azure Global and Azure China, multinational companies must often implement dual-stack networking architectures. One real-world case involved a global manufacturing company that needed to sync product data between its European headquarters and its China-based distribution centers. Since VPN tunnels into China must be provisioned through authorized telecom operators, and not all VPN protocols are permitted, they had to work with a licensed local ISP to deploy a regulatory-compliant Site-to-Site VPN from Frankfurt to China North 3, routing data through a DMZ with built-in latency buffers and caching.

Even within China, internet quality varies greatly by region. While Tier 1 cities like Beijing, Shanghai, and Shenzhen have world-class 5G and fiber networks, more rural provinces may experience network instability or constrained bandwidth. Azure China users should take this into account when deploying latency-sensitive services or selecting endpoints for IoT, media streaming, or financial transactions.

Finally, networking in China isn't just about routers and bandwidth it's also about relationships. In Chinese business culture, "guanxi" (关系), or personal relationships, often play a critical role in how quickly problems get resolved or how quickly infrastructure gets provisioned. It's not uncommon for a networking issue to require involvement from a local vendor's senior management to expedite resolution.

Building long-term partnerships with local managed service providers (MSPs), IT consultants, and cloud integrators is essential not just for deployment but also for long-term operations, compliance audits, and government filings.

Digital tools also matter. While LinkedIn is used, it is not the dominant business networking platform. WeChat is essential. It's not only a messaging platform but also a customer service tool, a payment interface, and a marketing channel. Most Azure China support teams including 21Vianet's technical team can be contacted through official WeChat accounts. Many Chinese enterprise cloud engineers will expect communication and even document sharing to happen there rather than over email.

Lesson 3

Monitoring, Management, and Automation Tools

In any modern cloud deployment, visibility and control are non-negotiables. But in the uniquely regulated and technically partitioned landscape of Azure China, monitoring, management, and automation tools serve an even more strategic role. For organizations operating in this sovereign cloud environment, the right tooling isn't just about keeping tabs on performance it's about ensuring regulatory compliance, maintaining operational resilience, and achieving scalability in a digital economy that moves at lightning speed.

Azure Monitor is at the core of the Azure China observability stack. It enables organizations to collect and analyze telemetry from applications, virtual machines, containers, and databases in near real-time. What makes Azure Monitor particularly valuable in the Chinese context is its localization. Operated by 21Vianet, the telemetry pipeline is hosted entirely within mainland China, which ensures compliance with data residency laws like the Cybersecurity Law and the Data Security Law. Businesses can use custom dashboards to visualize metrics such as CPU utilization, disk I/O latency, and memory usage across Availability Zones in China North 3, or monitor response time for critical web apps hosted in China East.

A regional logistics firm, for example, used Azure Monitor to track warehouse IoT data flowing into Azure Event Hubs. When latency spikes occurred, Azure Monitor sent alerts to their operations team, which automatically triggered runbooks via Azure Automation to reallocate processing capacity and stabilize throughput. This integration reduced downtime by over 60% in just two quarters.

But monitoring is only as effective as the system managing it. That's where Azure Resource Manager (ARM) comes into play. ARM provides a consistent deployment and management layer for Azure China resources, supporting JSON templates and API-based orchestration. It enables infrastructure-as-code practices, which are essential for scaling operations efficiently. In a region where service parity may lag behind global Azure, ARM also helps companies standardize environments across dev, staging, and production with a clear audit trail.

Through tagging and role-based access control (RBAC), enterprises can enforce compliance by region, team, or application type critical for multi-department operations or regulated sectors like finance and healthcare.

For example, a multinational financial firm running separate workloads in Azure China and Azure Global used ARM templates to mirror their architecture between regions while ensuring no data flowed across boundaries. This was essential not only for compliance but for disaster recovery simulations, allowing the company to maintain global architectural standards without violating China's strict data sovereignty rules.

Automation, too, plays a critical role in Azure China, especially where operational overhead is high and skilled cloud engineers may be scarce. Azure Automation allows teams to create and execute runbooks for common administrative tasks such as patching VMs, restarting services, or rotating secrets stored in Azure Key Vault. In China, where local holidays and regulatory audits can delay manual processes, automation becomes a competitive differentiator. Enterprises leveraging PowerShell DSC or Python scripts within Automation reduce errors and accelerate response times to events flagged by Azure Monitor alerts. One tech startup in Shanghai used runbooks to scale out virtual machines in response to API traffic surges from their mobile app, saving thousands of RMB per month by scaling back services during off-peak hours.

But it's not just about Microsoft-native tooling. Many enterprises complement Azure's built-in capabilities with tools like Azure Security Center and Azure Advisor both available in Azure China to receive actionable recommendations on performance, cost, and security. Azure Security Center in particular offers policy-driven governance and threat detection that aligns with local compliance frameworks such as MLPS 2.0 (Multi-Level Protection Scheme). Combined with Azure Monitor logs, this provides end-to-end observability, from performance tuning to intrusion detection.

Third-party integrations are increasingly common in Azure China, too. Solutions such as Grafana for visualization, or Terraform (when hosted on-prem or via a local CI/CD pipeline) can be used to extend observability and configuration management. However, it's important to note that not all global services are available in China.

For instance, Microsoft Sentinel and Log Analytics may have delayed or limited functionality, requiring alternative logging strategies or hybrid deployments with locally hosted SIEM platforms.

As more businesses adopt containerization in China, tools like Azure Kubernetes Service (AKS) also bring their own monitoring challenges. Integrating container insights with Azure Monitor enables real-time visibility into pod performance, node health, and cluster capacity, all within the boundaries of Chinese regulatory compliance. Automation, in this context, extends to Helm chart deployments, CI/CD integrations, and policy enforcement via Azure Policy another important tool for maintaining consistency and compliance across scaled environments.

CHAPTER 7
BEST PRACTICES AND FUTURE OUTLOOK

Lesson 1

Best Practices for Success in Azure China

Succeeding in Azure China is not simply about applying global cloud strategies in a new location it's about adapting them to one of the world's most complex digital environments. Azure China operates as a sovereign cloud, licensed by Microsoft and run independently by 21Vianet, and it demands a deep understanding of both technical architecture and regulatory nuance. Organizations that thrive in this market are those that localize their cloud thinking from day one, aligning their infrastructure, compliance, partnerships, and cultural approach to the realities of operating in China.

The starting point for any Azure China initiative is compliance. Laws such as the Cybersecurity Law, Data Security Law, and Personal Information Protection Law (PIPL) shape everything from data residency to application architecture. Foreign companies must ensure that personal data collected within China stays within Chinese borders and that any cross-border data transfers go through regulatory review. It's no longer enough to encrypt and anonymize you must demonstrate clear control over data flows, storage locations, and access privileges. Businesses entering China should work with local legal advisors who understand the evolving regulatory frameworks and can guide on sector-specific compliance (e.g., MLPS 2.0 in finance or telecoms).

Beyond compliance, technical design choices play a decisive role. Azure China does not support direct integration with global Azure, meaning hybrid cloud or multi-region solutions must be carefully designed. Services like Azure Arc, Azure Stack, or third-party synchronization tools become critical to bridge gaps between your international and Chinese deployments. Some organizations even maintain parallel CI/CD pipelines one for global Azure, and another for Azure China hosted entirely onshore to ensure consistency and code parity without violating data laws. A standout best practice is to adopt a China-first infrastructure model. For example, a global healthcare SaaS company deployed its entire front-end and data layer in China North 3, using Azure CDN (China) with integration to WeChat Mini Programs for native user experience.

Their backend microservices were mirrored with global counterparts, but authentication and storage remained fully inside China to ensure compliance. This approach not only minimized latency but also gained regulatory approvals much faster than traditional hybrid models that relied on overseas service components.

Localization doesn't stop at infrastructure. To succeed in Azure China, you need to localize your application and user experience as well. This means integrating with popular Chinese platforms Alipay and WeChat Pay for payments, Baidu Maps instead of Google Maps, SMS via Chinese telecom providers instead of Twilio, and login integrations with WeChat or local identity providers. Localization also includes adhering to UI/UX expectations in Chinese applications, which often feature denser interfaces, mobile-first workflows, and embedded social features. By adapting your service model to local consumer behavior, businesses can drive higher adoption and retention rates.

Building local partnerships is another key success factor. In China, guanxi (关系) personal and professional relationships matters as much as technical excellence. Establishing relationships with licensed local ISVs, MSPs, and cloud-native consultancies accelerates regulatory filings, ICP license applications, and Azure onboarding. These partners often have direct lines to provincial regulators or data center operations, which can shorten your go-to-market timelines significantly. Some foreign enterprises even embed bilingual cloud architects or DevOps engineers within their China teams to bridge cultural and technical gaps.

Training is also an underestimated area. Azure China evolves differently from global Azure. Services may launch later, documentation might be partially translated, and updates may follow different cycles. Organizations should prioritize region-specific Azure certifications, and assign team members to track changes in China-specific service availability via the official regional services list. Some companies set up monthly review calls between their global and China IT teams just to stay aligned on service parity and deployment limitations.

Once your architecture is live, monitoring and optimization must become continuous. Azure Monitor, Application Insights, and Cost Management tools are available in China, but default configurations must be adjusted to use China-based endpoints. Setting up detailed alert rules for latency spikes, DNS resolution failures, and ExpressRoute performance can dramatically reduce downtime.

Enterprises should schedule quarterly cloud audits to identify orphaned resources, inefficient scaling strategies, or noncompliant service configurations. One financial services firm saved over ¥120,000 RMB annually by using Azure Advisor in China to identify underutilized reserved instances and restructure their VNet topology for cross-region billing optimization.

Lastly, success in Azure China is a long game. Organizations that invest in localized governance models, hire bilingual cloud leaders, and maintain a pulse on regulatory shifts will consistently outperform those that treat China as just another deployment zone. Success isn't just technical it's legal, cultural, and operational.

Lesson 2

Emerging Trends in the Chinese Cloud Market

The Chinese cloud computing market is no longer simply growing—it's undergoing a profound transformation, positioning itself as one of the most sophisticated and regulated digital ecosystems in the world. With revenues surpassing $48 billion USD in 2023, China is the second-largest cloud market globally, behind only the United States. However, unlike in other markets, success in China hinges not just on scale or technical capability, but on navigating a constantly shifting landscape of government policy, local innovation, digital sovereignty, and consumer expectations.

One of the most defining trends is the continued dominance of local cloud providers, including Alibaba Cloud, Huawei Cloud, Tencent Cloud, and more recently China Telecom Cloud. These companies collectively hold over 75% of the market share, with Alibaba alone accounting for nearly 32%, according to IDC China. These providers aren't just expanding their infrastructure footprint they're building industry-specific solutions for manufacturing, fintech, retail, and healthcare, and aligning tightly with national priorities like "New Infrastructure" (新基建) and "Made in China 2025". International providers such as Microsoft Azure (via 21Vianet) must therefore offer differentiated value, such as global compliance frameworks, enterprise security models, and hybrid deployment capabilities, to stay relevant and complementary in this competitive arena.

A second major trend is the mainstream adoption of hybrid and multi-cloud strategies. Chinese enterprises, especially in regulated industries like finance, energy, and government services, are increasingly deploying hybrid architectures that balance public cloud scalability with on-premise or private cloud control. This is largely driven by regulations such as the Multi-Level Protection Scheme (MLPS 2.0), which restricts how and where data can be stored and accessed. In practice, this has led to a rise in cloud-native solutions deployed on Azure Stack, on-prem Kubernetes clusters, or with region-specific compliance wrappers.

For Azure China users, hybrid cloud adoption is further accelerated by the lack of direct interoperability between Azure Global and Azure China.

A growing number of enterprises now deploy duplicate environments, connected by ExpressRoute, authorized MPLS tunnels, or content delivery strategies that comply with local cross-border data controls. Global CIOs now recognize that success in China often requires a parallel digital strategy, one that mirrors architecture but localizes operations, data, and governance.

Meanwhile, AI and big data are reshaping the purpose of the cloud itself. According to a 2023 China AI Development Report, over 60% of Chinese enterprises have already deployed AI applications in production environments many of them powered through cloud platforms. Local providers are leading in consumer-facing AI (such as NLP, recommendation engines, and real-time video analytics), while global players like Microsoft are differentiating through enterprise AI frameworks, responsible AI governance, and model interpretability areas highly relevant to multinationals operating in China.

In Azure China, services like Azure Machine Learning, Azure Databricks (in limited preview), and AI-based APIs are gaining traction, especially among local startups and R&D divisions of global companies. However, Azure China's AI roadmap tends to lag the global release cycle, prompting cloud architects to adopt hybrid AI strategies, where training may happen in global environments, but inference and model deployment are localized within China.

Perhaps the most critical trend shaping the Chinese cloud market is the tightening of regulatory oversight not just in terms of data residency, but in algorithm governance, AI ethics, cybersecurity ratings, and cross-border compliance. Laws such as the Data Security Law, Personal Information Protection Law (PIPL), and the newly enforced Cross-Border Data Transfer Security Assessment Measures (2022) fundamentally influence how foreign firms design, operate, and govern their cloud systems.

Azure China addresses these challenges through a sovereign operations model where Microsoft licenses its technology to 21Vianet, who independently owns and operates the infrastructure. This model ensures legal and operational separation from global Azure, but it also places greater responsibility on customers to understand which services are available, which regions are permitted for certain workloads, and how local governance processes—like obtaining an ICP license or completing a security classification filing can affect their rollout timelines.

Lastly, green cloud computing and carbon neutrality are emerging themes in China's cloud discourse. The Chinese government has committed to peaking carbon emissions by 2030 and achieving carbon neutrality by 2060. In response, local cloud providers are building carbon-tracking dashboards, renewable-powered data centers, and sustainability APIs. Azure China is also participating in this transition, with Microsoft's broader commitment to becoming carbon negative by 2030 gradually making its way into the China roadmap.

Lesson 3

Advice for IT Professionals and Enterprises

Navigating Azure China is more than a matter of deploying infrastructure it requires a well-informed, agile strategy that bridges global best practices with the realities of the Chinese regulatory and technical landscape. For IT professionals and enterprises, success lies in localizing your approach while retaining your global standards, particularly when it comes to compliance, architecture, innovation, and team development.

The regulatory environment in China continues to evolve rapidly, and ignoring it is not an option. Laws such as the Cybersecurity Law, Data Security Law, and the Personal Information Protection Law (PIPL) impose strict rules on how data is collected, stored, processed, and transferred. These regulations aren't just paperwork they define where your data can reside, who can access it, and how systems must be architected. For example, multinational companies operating in Azure China must ensure data residency within China, meaning that even centralized logging or analytics tools must be fully localized. Cross-border data flows require not only encryption but also a government-approved security assessment, which can delay rollout timelines by weeks or months. To stay ahead, IT leaders should maintain a direct line of communication with local legal advisors and assign compliance champions within their cloud teams.

Security, meanwhile, is a shared responsibility, but Azure China customers must take more ownership than in global Azure. While the underlying infrastructure is managed by 21Vianet, configuration of all cloud workloads is your responsibility. Security misconfigurations are one of the leading causes of breaches globally, and China is no exception. A robust cloud security posture must start with Azure Active Directory (China), Network Security Groups, and Key Vault, but go further to include zero-trust architectures, multi-factor authentication (MFA), and role-based access control (RBAC). Azure Security Center (available in China) offers helpful baselines and vulnerability scanning, while manual audits should still be performed quarterly, particularly in industries subject to MLPS 2.0 or financial regulation. One of the most underestimated success factors in Azure China is building strong local partnerships.

One of the most underestimated success factors in Azure China is building strong local partnerships. Whether you're deploying a multi-region web app or an IoT platform across industrial sites, local system integrators and cloud-native partners will often provide crucial services that Microsoft or 21Vianet cannot. For instance, obtaining an ICP license to operate a public-facing website in China requires coordination with local telecom providers. Partnering with a certified Azure China MSP can help accelerate licensing, procurement, support, and even ExpressRoute provisioning. In addition, these partners are often deeply familiar with regional connectivity challenges, CDN options, and data protection obligations. These relationships often extend beyond technical support—they provide guanxi (关系), the local trust and access required to solve regulatory or operational roadblocks.

For forward-looking enterprises, Azure China is not just a compliance puzzle—it's also a platform for innovation. Services such as Azure Machine Learning, Cognitive Services, and AI-driven search and translation APIs are increasingly available within China and can unlock powerful capabilities for local personalization, intelligent automation, and predictive analytics. One Chinese retail brand used Azure AI to build a recommendation engine tailored for WeChat Mini Programs, increasing conversion rates by 18% in just two quarters. To harness these services, IT professionals must stay ahead of Azure China's service availability roadmap and proactively plan for service gaps or release delays relative to global Azure. Some enterprises implement shadow deployments globally to test cutting-edge services, while using Azure China as their operational backbone—balancing innovation with compliance.

Upskilling your team is non-negotiable. Azure evolves rapidly—and Azure China evolves differently. IT professionals must be aware of not just service features but local implementation nuances, such as differences in endpoints, authentication flows, and PowerShell command parameters. Training programs should include region-specific certifications, like "Architecting on Azure China," and encourage bilingual documentation and toolchain management. Organizations that establish internal Azure China champions— engineers or architects who own the local stack—see far higher success rates and faster problem resolution.

Finally, resource optimization is key to sustainable operations. Azure China provides tools like Azure Cost Management, Azure Monitor, and Advisor, but these tools often require additional tuning for localized environments. For example, global budget alerts or Azure Policy scripts may not directly translate to the China cloud due to API endpoint differences.

A manufacturing company running data-heavy AI workloads in China East 2 saved over ¥200,000 RMB annually by right-sizing its VM instances and switching to reserved instance pricing models based on Advisor recommendations. Organizations should schedule monthly governance reviews to evaluate spend, performance, and compliance metrics—and adjust resource allocation accordingly.

CHAPTER 8
CASE STUDIES AND SUCCESS STORIES

Case Study 1: Optimizing Content Delivery with Azure China's CDN

A global video streaming platform expanding into China needed to optimize content delivery for users across different regions. They initially planned to use Azure Front Door, but upon realizing it was unavailable in Azure China, they faced issues with high latency and buffering problems for Chinese users.

Solution:

Instead of relying on a third-party CDN, the company utilized Azure China's CDN, which integrates with multiple local CDN vendors to deliver optimized content per region. They hosted their video assets in Azure Blob Storage and leveraged Azure China's Smart Route technology to automatically choose the most efficient CDN provider based on geographic location. This resulted in a 40% improvement in video load times, enhancing user experience.

Case Study 2: Establishing a Low-Latency ExpressRoute Connection

A global automotive manufacturer operating smart factories in China needed a low-latency and high-reliability network connection between their multiple production sites. However, with Azure China's infrastructure isolated from the global Azure network, they needed a secure and compliant solution.

Solution:

The company deployed Azure ExpressRoute in China, taking advantage of Azure China's free ExpressRoute circuit between China North and China North 2, as well as China East and China East 2. This minimized latency and eliminated costs associated with inter-region traffic, allowing them to process IoT data in near real-time. By leveraging ExpressRoute Premium for cross-region connectivity, they successfully connected factories across the country while ensuring full compliance with China's regulatory requirements.

Case Study 3: Complying with China's Data Residency Laws

A multinational financial institution wanted to deploy its customer analytics and fraud detection system in China. However, they had concerns about compliance with China's Cybersecurity Law and Multi-Level Protection Scheme (MLPS 2.0), which require sensitive financial data to be stored locally.

Solution:

The company set up Azure SQL Database and Azure Synapse Analytics in Azure China regions to process customer transactions locally. They also used Azure Key Vault to store encryption keys within China, ensuring that no sensitive financial data left the country. By following MLPS compliance guidelines and using Azure Security Center, they maintained a secure, compliant, and scalable cloud infrastructure for their financial operations.

Case Study 4: Deploying AI Models with Azure Machine Learning

A Chinese AI startup specializing in facial recognition wanted to use Azure Machine Learning to train deep learning models. However, some AI services in Azure Global, such as Azure OpenAI, were unavailable in Azure China.

Solution:

To adapt, the startup trained its AI models on-premises using Azure Stack Hub and then deployed them on Azure Kubernetes Service (AKS) in China. They used Azure Machine Learning service within China to manage and automate model retraining while ensuring full compliance with China's AI and data governance regulations.

Case Study 5: Hybrid Cloud Strategy for a Retail Business

A European retail company expanding into China needed a hybrid cloud solution that could integrate its on-premises SAP system with Azure China. Since Azure China is completely isolated from global Azure regions, direct data synchronization was not possible.

Solution:

They deployed Azure Stack Hub in China to host SAP workloads on-premises while using Azure Arc to extend their cloud operations into Azure China North and China East regions. This hybrid solution allowed them to maintain centralized inventory tracking, process local transactions, and integrate global reporting without violating China's data sovereignty laws.

Case Study 6: Hosting Multiplayer Gaming Servers with Low Latency

A gaming company needed to host multiplayer game servers in China while maintaining low latency for real-time player interactions.

Solution:

They migrated their backend game servers to Azure China's Ningxia and Shanghai regions, utilizing Azure Traffic Manager to route players to the nearest available server. Additionally, they used Azure Redis Cache for real-time session storage, reducing server response times by 50% and significantly improving gameplay experiences.

Case Study 7: Blockchain Compliance in China

A European blockchain company wanted to offer enterprise blockchain solutions to its Chinese clients but faced regulatory hurdles, as China heavily regulates decentralized networks.

Solution:

They built a private blockchain network using Hyperledger Fabric on Azure Kubernetes Service (AKS) in China, ensuring that all nodes operated within China's legal framework. This approach allowed them to comply with Chinese blockchain regulations while still offering secure, decentralized solutions for enterprise clients.

Case Study 8: Securing Healthcare Data Under China's Regulations

An international healthcare provider needed to store and process sensitive patient data in China while ensuring compliance with China's data protection laws.

Solution:

They implemented Azure Synapse Analytics and Azure SQL Database in Azure China, ensuring that all sensitive patient records remained within the country. Using Azure Virtual WAN, they established a secure network between their Azure China infrastructure and on-premises hospital systems, allowing data to remain secure while still being accessible for research and analysis.

Case Study 9: IoT Deployment for a Smart Manufacturing Firm

A global manufacturing company deploying smart factory solutions in China needed a real-time IoT data processing system to optimize production.

Solution:

They implemented Azure IoT Hub and Azure Data Explorer in Azure China to process sensor data in real-time while ensuring compliance with China's industrial data laws. The new system improved production efficiency by 35% and reduced equipment downtime by predicting maintenance needs before failures occurred.

Case Study 10: Building a Cloud-Based ERP System for a Logistics Provider

A logistics firm needed a cloud-based ERP solution to optimize its supply chain in China, but Azure China's isolation from Azure Global made global data integration a challenge.

Solution:

The company deployed SAP on Azure Virtual Machines within Azure China and used Azure Arc for hybrid cloud management. They leveraged ExpressRoute and VPN Gateway to securely connect their Chinese operations with their global logistics network, ensuring seamless real-time tracking and reporting.

CHAPTER 9
RESOURCES AND RECOMMENDATIONS

Table of Useful Resources

Resource	Description	Link
Azure China Homepage	Official portal for Azure China services, pricing, and solutions	https://www.azure.cn/en-us/
Azure China Blog	Updates on new features, tools, and case studies for Azure China users.	https://www.azure.cn/en-us/pricing/
Azure China Pricing	Detailed pricing information for Azure services in China..	https://www.azure.cn/en-us/pricing/
Azure Events Portal	Register for webinars and events tailored for Azure China users.	https://chinaevent.microsoft.com/events/
Azure China Products	Documentation on popular Azure China services and configurations.	https://docs.azure.cn/en-us/?product=popular
Azure China Service Availability	A comprehensive overview of which Azure services are available in China.	https://learn.microsoft.com/en-us/azure/china/concepts-service-availability

Azure China Marketplace	A marketplace for finding third-party applications and solutions optimized for Azure China.	https://market.azure.cn/Home
Azure China Support Plans	Official Microsoft support options for Azure China, ranging from basic to enterprise-grade assistance.	https://support.azure.cn/en-us/support/plans/

CHAPTER 10
GLOSSARY OF KEY TERMS AND CONCEPTS

Terms	Description
Azure China	A separate instance of Microsoft Azure operated by 21Vianet in compliance with China's cloud regulations. It is completely isolated from Azure Global.
21Viane	The exclusive local partner operating Azure China under China's data sovereignty laws. It is responsible for managing cloud services within the country.
Azure China Regions	Azure China currently has three regions: China North, China East, and China North 3. These regions are separate from Azure Global and are required to comply with Chinese data residency laws.
Azure ExpressRoute	A private network connection between on-premises infrastructure and Azure China, reducing latency and improving security. Azure China offers free ExpressRoute circuits for paired regions (China North – China North 2, and China East – China East 2).
Azure Stack	Hub A hybrid cloud solution that allows organizations to deploy Azure services on-premises while maintaining integration with Azure China. Used for businesses needing strict data residency compliance.
Azure Virtual Network (VNet)	A logically isolated network in Azure China, used to securely connect cloud resources within the region's infrastructure. It does not have native connectivity to Azure Global VNets.

Multi-Level Protection Scheme (MLPS 2.0)	A Chinese cybersecurity regulation that requires IT systems including cloud environments to implement security controls based on their importance to national security. All cloud services hosted in China must comply.
ICP Filing (Internet Content Provider Filing)	registration required by the Chinese government for any website or service hosted on a China-based cloud (including Azure China) before it can be publicly accessible.
Azure China Service Availability	Microsoft provides a separate list of services available in Azure China, as not all Azure Global services are offered due to regulatory and localization constraints.

Azure China CDN	A content delivery network (CDN) service in Azure China that integrates with local Chinese CDN providers to optimize website and application performance across China.
Azure Security Center (China	A cloud security service that monitors Azure China environments, providing threat detection, compliance recommendations, and security posture assessments.
Azure Key Vault	A secure storage solution for encryption keys, secrets, and certificates, ensuring that sensitive data never leaves China while complying with Chinese data security laws.
Azure China Marketplace	A marketplace that provides third-party applications and services optimized for Azure China, ensuring compatibility with local regulations and business needs.
Azure China Support Plans	Microsoft offers separate support plans for Azure China, managed by 21Vianet, covering different service levels from basic to enterprise-grade assistance.
Azure API Management	A service enabling businesses to securely publish, manage, and monitor APIs in Azure China, ensuring compliance with Chinese integration policies.
Cross-Border Data Transfer Restrictions	A key regulation in China's Cybersecurity Law, restricting how data can be transferred out of China, requiring businesses to store and process sensitive data locally within Azure China regions.
Hybrid Cloud Strategy	A common deployment model where enterprises use Azure Stack Hub or Azure Arc to extend their global cloud presence into China while ensuring compliance with data residency laws.
Azure Traffic Manager (China)	A load balancing service that allows businesses to route users to the nearest Azure China region, improving application performance within China's regulatory environment.

| Azure China VPN Gateway | A service that provides a secure site-to-site VPN connection between on-premises networks and Azure China Virtual Networks (VNets). This is required since Azure China is fully isolated from Azure Global. |

Azure Portal	The dedicated web interface for managing Azure China services, located at https://portal.azure.cn, separate from the global Azure portal.
Azure China CDN	Azure's content delivery network offering within China that leverages local CDN vendors (e.g., ChinaCache, Wangsu) to deliver content efficiently and in compliance with local regulations.
Azure China Trial Account	A temporary Azure China account available by request, typically providing up to $500 USD worth of usage credit and valid for two months. Requires a Chinese business license.
PIPL (Personal Information Protection Law)	A major data privacy regulation in China, similar to GDPR, that governs how personal data is collected, stored, and used within the country. Azure China services must adhere to this framework.
China DR Region	Disaster recovery region designated for a primary Azure China region, such as China East 3 for China North 3. Not publicly available and used only for redundancy.

www.ingramcontent.com/pod-product-compliance
Lightning Source LLC
LaVergne TN
LVHW051707050326
832903LV00032B/4058